T0063465

12

SECRETS TO A
MIRACLE-WORKING FAITH

INCREASE YOUR ABILITY TO RECEIVE
MIRACLES FROM GOD

VICTOR N. ALVAREZ

WESTBOW
PRESS
A DIVISION OF THOMAS NELSON

Scriptures taken from THE HOLY BIBLE containing the OLD and NEW Testaments in the King James Version, *Power Publishing, Corp.* P.O. box 127 McDonald, TN. 37353 Copyright 2006.

WestBow Press books may be ordered through booksellers or by contacting:

WestBow Press
A Division of Thomas Nelson
1663 Liberty Drive
Bloomington, IN 47403
www.westbowpress.com
1 (866) 928-1240

ISBN: 978-1-4908-1638-8 (sc)
ISBN: 978-1-4908-1639-5 (e)

Library of Congress Control Number: 2013921397

Printed in the United States of America.

WestBow Press rev. date: 12/20/2013

Promotional Picture used for flyers

(Victor Alvarez and Jim Alvarez preaching
over the radio in Costa Rica, ca. 1986)

Contents

Acknowledgments

First of all, I'd like to thank the greatest contributor in the production of this book. Of course I am talking about the Holy Spirit; it would have been impossible to produce this book without His revelation, guidance, and orientation about the sequence of the chapters. Thank You, Holy Spirit, and to God be the glory.

I would also like to thank Rachel Alvarez, my daughter. Without her input and observations in revising the manuscript, it would have been almost impossible to complete this book in its present format. Thank you, Rachel. I am grateful to you.

I would also like to thank Cristian Bermudez for his invaluable contribution in revising the editing and lexicon of the manuscripts. To him, I am immensely grateful. His patience and understanding helped me in the production of the book.

I would also like to thank my son, John Alvarez, for his contribution in the writing of the manuscripts.

I am totally grateful to the persons mentioned above, and I thank the Holy Spirit for bringing them into my life at the appropriate times and circumstances.

Dedication

With all of my love, I dedicate this book to my Lord Jesus. I owe it all to Him. Without His sacrifice, I wouldn't have salvation or the revelation of the Holy Spirit to speak about the subject. Thanks to the Lord; His mercy and grace endure forever.

Secondly, I dedicate this book to the readers. You may be of different nationalities, levels of education, and social statuses, but you all have one thing in common: you are hungry for the Word of God. May this book on faith be a blessing to you and help you satisfy your spiritual hunger.

(Auditorium Meeting in Miami, 1995)

Preface

Dear Reader:

It is my most fervent prayer that *"12 Secrets to a Miracle Working Faith" / "Develop Your Ability to Receive Miracles from God"* results in a revolutionary spiritual growth in your understanding of faith and your ability to receive miracles from God.

I want to congratulate you for acquiring this book, because it is an indication that you are truly seeking to learn more about faith.

'Without faith it is impossible to please God' [Hebrews 11:6: (KJV Holy Bible, *2006 Power Publishing Corp.*)]. In order to have God pleased with you, you do not need a good reputation, money, nobility, or a high level of education: all you need is some good old-fashioned faith.

Your faith will catch His attention. He is willing to dialogue with you if you have faith. Nothing can give you favor with God as a little faith could, even if it is as small as the seed of a mustard tree. You should try it because it works.

Even though this book is a summarized overview of faith, we have attempted to make it as spiritually profound and biblically sound as possible. We do not presume or pretend that this practical application for daily living be considered as a theological treatise on the matter, but rather as a layman's introductory guide on the topic of faith.

Perhaps you have been exposed to the subject already, but deep in your heart, you want to learn more about it, because you need a miracle from God—and you need it now. If this is you, this book has been written with you in mind.

May this book bless your life and be a guide in your journey toward the miracle land, the place where God reigns.

(Victor preaching via radio in San Jose, Costa Rica, ca. 1986)

Disclaimer

We (the author, the publishing company, and the sales agents of this product) do not warrant in any way, shape, or form that everybody who comes in contact with the contents of this book will receive a miracle from God. The answer to prayers is entirely up to God's discretion. Only He knows the intricacies of the human heart and the complexity of the circumstances surrounding the life of the person seeking a miracle.

Some will receive miracles, and some will not. His answer may not be a final "no", but He may say, "No, not now."

Ultimately, the answer to your request is in His hands and no one else's.

If you receive it, praise the Lord. If you do not, do not be discouraged.

Introduction

I have written this book as an expression of my personal experience with the GOD of Miracles. After traveling extensively throughout many countries and states, and preaching the gospel "to every creature" via radio and television—under tents, in the open air, in churches, in jails, and in auditoriums—I have witnessed the power of GOD in effect, as it works miracles for multitudes of people.

In my ministerial experience, I discovered that the common denominator of the people who received miracles was that they had faith. "Without faith, it is impossible to please God" [Hebrews 11:6(KJV Holy Bible, *2006 Power Publishing Corp.*)]. **I have decided to share this experience with the conviction and assurance of my witnessing others exercising their faith, and my personal experience using my faith to receive miracles from the Almighty**.

Twelve Secrets to a Miracle-Working Faith: Develop Your Ability to Receive Miracles from God is a compacted form of the many lectures and messages I have delivered on the topic of faith. I believe that your understanding of faith and the principles that rule the exercising of faith will be decisive in the development of your faith and consequently in you receiving miracles from God.

Faith has a Prerequisite

It is important to note that faith has a prerequisite. True faith cannot be obtained unless we make a commitment to God. By this, I mean that when we approach God in search of a miracle, we must believe, first of all, that there is a God. 'Whosoever comes to GOD must believe that GOD is the rewarder of those who diligently seek Him' [Heb. 11:6 (KJV Holy Bible, *2006 Power Publishing Corp.*)].

We must believe that GOD is our Creator and our Father and that He sent His only beloved Son, Jesus Christ, to die on Calvary for the redemption of humanity. We must also believe that Jesus rose from the dead on the third day and that He ascended into heaven. We must believe that Jesus is the only way to the Father. We must accept Jesus as our personal Savior and Lord.

Do you believe this? Are you willing to accept Him as your Savior? The Bible says that if you believe with all your heart and confess with your mouth, you shall be saved. "Blessed … are those who seek Him with the whole heart" [Psalms119:2b (KJV Holy Bible, *2006 Power Publishing Corp.*)].

Let us go into His presence by way of prayer and repeat this prayer of salvation:

(Tent Revival in Guatemala, ca. 1987)

Dear Father in heaven, I come before you to tell you that I am sorry for my sins. I want you to wash me in the blood of your beloved Son, Jesus Christ, who died for me on the cross. I accept His payment for my sins, and I receive Him as my Lord and Savior. I declare that I will live for Him from this day on. I declare that I am a new creature and that I am born again. I die to my sinful life, and I am ready to live for you, from this day on.
In Jesus' name: amen.

Congratulations, my friend, if you have just prayed this prayer—for this is the prayer of salvation. This experience constitutes the greatest miracle you can receive. Any other miracles are small by comparison. After all, we are talking about knowing God on a personal level. You will not have to spend eternity in the lake of fire. Instead, you are going to heaven, and you will spend all of eternity with God. Thank God for your salvation. Amen. Praise the Lord.

Now that you have fulfilled the prerequisite, you are ready to proceed with the subject of faith. God knows that you are not looking for Him because you only want a miracle out of Him; it is because you love Him and have a relationship with Him. You have a right to partake of His blessings and riches, which is to partake of the bread of His children. Without further ado, let us get into the subject matter.

(Baptism service in Houston, ca. 1984)

A Vision of the Cross

For the first time in my life
My eyes were opened.
I had a vision of Christ hung on the cross,
Dying for us: for you and for me.
It broke my heart to see Him there.
I saw his face,
Bloody and disfigured.
I saw His body savagely wounded,
The surface of His skin covered in red.
His hands and feet driven by nails:
I saw His agony and despair.
His butchered body hanging there,
Paying for sins He did not commit
Accepting the penalty for sins that were not his
O, yes, I saw Him crying to the Father.
His tears contained His love and care,
The crown of thorns wounding His forehead,
The running streams of blood being shed for me.
I saw the Prince of Peace dying so restlessly,
The healer of humanity consumed by sickness,
The author of life subjected to death.
I saw Him whispering to His Father,
"Do not impute this sin to them.
Forgive them, for they do not know what they have done."

"It is finished," He said.
Then, a silence came.
Thank you, dear Father, for salvation.
I don't have to go to hell. I am heaven-bound.
Thank you, Lord, for reconciliation.
Your favor and grace, in Christ I've found.

(Community meeting in Guatemala, ca. 1988)

A Doctrinal Declaration of Faith

I declare that I believe in God, our Heavenly Father. I believe that at an appointed time, He sent His Son, Jesus, to be the perfect sacrifice and to shed His blood on the cross of Calvary for the forgiveness of our sins, for our healing, and for a God-sent prosperity. I believe that Jesus was resurrected from the tomb on the third day and that soon after his resurrection; He ascended into the heavens where He is interceding for all believers. I believe He defeated the devil and the power of death and now holds the keys to hell and death.

Those who, by faith, have accepted Jesus are saved and have become a nation of priests, dedicated fully to His service. I believe that Jesus sent His Holy Spirit to dwell in His church and that the church is empowered to do the same miracles, signs, and wonders that Jesus did. He is the same yesterday, today, and forever. I believe the Bible is the inspired Word of God, good for the guidance and instruction of all humanity.

I believe that Jesus will come back for the second time with the sound of the trumpet and pick up His church. At His return, the dead in Christ will rise again, and those who are alive will be transformed into a glorified body in the twinkle of an eye. And so, we shall be with the Lord forevermore.

So I believe, according to God's Word.

(Altar Ministry San Antonio, TX. USA ca. 1995)

SECRET I

Faith Is Not Mental Assent

What is a mental assent? To have mental assent means to experience a belief with the mind only. That kind of belief does not go deep enough into the heart to produce a miracle in the life.

It is possible for God to perform a miracle—and just leave it at that. As you can see, mental assent is only an approval of the mind about the possibility that God may perform miracles. Mental assent is the first stage on the journey to the City of Miracles.

'For out of the heart flow the springs of life: blessings, miracles [Prov. 4:23, (KJV Holy Bible, *2006 Power Publishing Corp.*)]. Let's talk about what that means. Suppose you get very sick, and no matter what you do, your situation grows worse. You realize that only a miracle from God will help. You realize that a deeper kind of faith is required; your mind must agree about the possibility that God may heal you. As a result, you go to a deeper level of faith; you engage your heart into believing that you will receive a miracle. You begin to confess the promises of God regarding healing, and you are expecting God to heal you. You believe with your mind—and with your heart. You have the certainty that God will perform a miracle. You have gone beyond the limitations of mental assent. If such is the case, then 'keep thy heart diligent for out of it (heart, spirit) issue the springs of life (healing)' has been fulfilled [Prov. 4:23, (KJV Holy Bible, *2006 Power Publishing Corp.*)].

"For with heart you believe unto righteousness, and with the mouth confession is made unto salvation" [Rom. 10:10 (KJV Holy Bible, *2006 Power Publishing Corp.*)]. When the Bible says "with the heart," it also means "with the spirit." God is a spirit; in order to relate to Him, we must relate to Him on a spiritual level.

The Bible says that God created humans in His image (see Gen. 1:26). ***The image of God in man means that God, aside from giving people bodies and souls, also gave them spirits***. So then, a person is a spirit who has a soul and lives within a body. A person uses his or her body to relate to the physical realm. People use the soul (the depository of their lives, wills, emotions, and intellects) and relate to the physical or natural realm through the senses. With the spirit, a person can relate to the spiritual realm. It is important to understand that the spiritual realm is just as real as the physical one—even though it is invisible to the human eye.

God is 'looking for worshippers who want to worship Him in "spirit and in truth"'[John 4:23, (KJV Holy Bible, *2006 Power Publishing Corp.*)] Therefore, we may conclude that in order to receive a miracle, you must give your mental assent (soul) and believe with your heart (spirit).

Are you ready to go beyond your intelligence, your mind, and believe with your heart? If that is the case, let us go beyond the second stage on the journey toward the City of Faith where you will receive your miracle.

To exercise your faith, I want you to declare in a loud voice:

> I declare that I believe in God. I also believe in Jesus. He is my Lord and Savior. I believe that He died to pay for my sins, and that by His stripes I am healed. I declare that I believe not only with my mind but also with all my heart in Him and his Word. I believe all His promises are true. I declare that His grace and favor are operating in my life— and that He has made supernatural provision for all my needs. I declare that all of God's blessings are upon me and that this day is a blessed day.
>
> In the name of Jesus: amen, and amen.

(Open air street meeting in Guatemala, ca. 1986)

SECRET II

Faith Activates the Spiritual Senses

One of humanity's two dimensions is earthly, or physical. It relates to the natural environment (the sun, rain, food, etc.). In this dimension, people interact with their surroundings (the earth).

The other dimension is spiritual; a person is a spirit who has a soul and lives within a body. To relate to the natural environment, or physical realm, a person uses his or her natural senses: touch, smell, sight, taste, and hearing. To relate to the spiritual realm, a person uses his or her spiritual senses, which are part of the spiritual body. These correspond to the natural senses, but they operate in the spiritual realm.

To operate in the physical realm, the mind activates the physical organs (eyes, nose, hands, mouth, and ears). Likewise, the spirit has spiritual senses to relate to the spiritual realm. These can be activated by faith. Thus, people may operate in both realms. Jesus explains this in the parable of Lazarus and the rich man (see Luke 16:19–31). Lazarus was a beggar, and the rich man enjoyed everything in life. They both died and went onto paradise. In paradise, there was a great divide, and the rich man went to the depths of despair in hell. Lazarus went to the place of the righteous (heaven). The rich man was tormented by fire and felt the heat and thirst that came with the torments of hell.

The rich man asked God to send Lazarus to moisten the tip of his tongue with water because he could not take it anymore. As we can see here the senses of the spirit are being used even beyond death. Even though their bodies were dead and their physical organs were not functioning, they still could see each other. They could still hear and feel the environment. What does this have to do with faith?

"Now faith is the substance of things hoped for; the evidence of things not seen [Hebrews 11:1 (KJV Holy Bible, *2006 Power Publishing Corp.*)]. Clearer, faith is the assurance or confirmation for things one expects to receive from GOD, even though one has not experienced it with their physical senses! The things we hope for are miracles; or are revelations; or are other intangible things. Faith gives us the assurance, the conviction, and the certainty that what we are hoping for—the miracles we are expecting—are already a reality. Even though we do not perceive them with our physical senses, by faith, we perceive them as concrete facts.

By faith, we can accept their reality and await the manifestation of it in the physical realm. Faith is like a title, deed, or a certificate of ownership. It is proof that we have possession of a miracle even before it is manifested in the physical realm. To prove that I own a house, I do not have to walk around carrying the house over my shoulders. It is enough that I present my certificate of ownership to whoever is concerned to demonstrate that I am the owner of the property.

Show the devil your certificate, title, or deed and tell him that you have your miracle by faith. Your faith is your title or deed to healing; a car; a house; a job; salvation for a son or daughter; or whatever you need from the Lord. Claim it—and see it materialize. We can only experience this with our spiritual senses, through faith.

By faith, Abraham became a father at almost one hundred years old. He was almost as good as dead, but he became a "father of many nations" through his son(s) [Gen.17 (KJV Holy Bible, *2006 Power Publishing Corp.*)]. Angels came to visit his wife and him to announce to them that she was going to conceive a child within one year. Sarah laughed at first; she must have thought that God had a sense of humor because of how old she was. How could she, being old as she was, conceive a child? "By faith she received strength in her womb to conceive" [Heb. 11:11(KJV Holy Bible, *2006 Power Publishing Corp.*)]. After a year, she gave birth to Isaac—even though she was well beyond childbearing age. She was ninety years old when she had Isaac.

By faith, Abraham received the Promised Land. The Bible says he used to sojourn the land as a pilgrim. He did not even have a lot to bury his loved ones because the land belonged to some other nation, but he believed God was going to give him the territory. Trusting in God's promise, he used to greet the land from far away. He expected to possess it, and he and his descendants eventually did.

By faith, Moses threw his rod before the Pharaoh, and it became a snake. When the witch doctors of the king reproduced the miracle, Moses' snake swallowed the other snakes. Pharaoh was surprised to see the power of the God of Moses and had to understand that he was dealing with a god that was far superior to his gods.

By faith, Moses wrought the ten plagues in Egypt. God told Moses to go meet Pharaoh at the Nile River. Moses shared God's message with Pharaoh: "Let my people go that they may hold a feast to me in the wilderness". This has said the Lord; 'so that you may know who Jehovah is'. But, Pharaoh did not listen [see Exodus 5 (KJV Holy Bible, *2006 Power Publishing Corp.*)].

> Moses – empowered by the Almighty GOD declared, 'I will touch the river with my rod, and the water shall become blood. All the fish will die, and the river will stink. The Egyptians will be nauseated if they drink the water' [Ex. 7:17–21 (KJV Holy Bible, *2006 Power Publishing Corp.*)]. The events happened just as Moses said. Moses was so strong in his faith that he knew God would honor him by doing whatever He (GOD) said He (GOD) would do. Moses realized that he was being used by God, as he wrought the ten plagues.

One after another, Moses wrought the ten plagues, but Pharaoh's heart was hardened. After each plague, he would not heed God's message. God used Moses to bring judgment on Egypt by turning the Nile River into blood, by summoning frogs, by causing severe pestilence to Egyptians via lice, flies, dead livestock, boils that left them immobile, hail and fire, locusts, darkness, and finally death to the FIRST BORN of their children [Ex. 8–11, 12:29–30 (KJV Holy Bible, *2006 Power Publishing Corp.*)].

God warned Pharaoh, but he was hardened until he could cope no more and behaved in accordance with God's will and power, finally letting the people of Israel go. Thus, Moses by faith delivered the nation of Israel after 430 years of slavery. It would have been only four hundred years as God had promised Abraham, but in 390 Moses unexpectedly took matters into his own hands (see Gen. 15:13KJV Holy Bible, *2006 Power Publishing Corp.*).Trying to protect his people, he killed an Egyptian guard, which caused him to go into exile for forty years to the land of Midian (see Ex. 2:12–15 KJV Holy Bible, *2006 Power Publishing Corp*). He knew he was called to lead the Children of God out of Egypt, but it wasn't the time yet. So, by his failure, the time of the exodus was delayed thirty years.

When the Pharaoh saw his slaves were gone, he wondered who was going to build his temples, statues, and civic buildings, and he changed his mind. He decided to take his army, go after the nation of Israel, and bring his slaves back (see Ex. 14 KJV Holy Bible, *2006 Power Publishing Corp*). When Moses saw the army approaching, he realized he had to act fast. The problem was that he had the Red Sea in front of them, and there was no way for the 2.5 million people and their possessions (cattle, jewelry, etc.) to cross the Red Sea unless God performed a miracle.

Thousands of soldiers on chariots were approaching them quickly. If they caught up to them, they would be brought back to slavery. Moses trusted in God. He took his rod in one hand and divided the Red Sea with the other. It separated into two walls of water, and the people of Israel crossed the Red Sea on the road of dry land that was between the walls of water. They could physically see the water suspended in the air. The fish were still moving in the water as if it was normal. They saw Pharaoh and his army tenaciously advancing toward them, but the miracle had happened, and the people were hurriedly crossing through the Red Sea.

When they arrived at the other side, they would be totally safe. Pharaoh decided that he was going to use the miracle for his own benefit and ordered his army to move fast and apprehend his slaves.   When Pharaoh was about to overtake them, and the last Israelites were about to finish crossing the Red Sea, the waters behind the Israelites subsided, and Pharaoh and his chariots drowned. Their violence and plans to re-enslave them perished with them; there was no more slavery for the Israelites. They were free at last. Their enemies had succumbed to the power of their God, Jehovah. By faith, Moses had perceived what God was going to do and acted out accordingly. Thus, the people of Israel were saved that day.

Whatever your need is, whatever miracle you need, whatever your Red Sea is, by faith, you will cross it. God will divide the waters, and you will go across it like on dry land.

By faith, David defeated the giant Goliath. Bible scholars call these giants the *Nephilim*. In the Old Testament, the oldest reference to the giants is in Genesis 6:1–6. They were men of great stature, ranging from eight to twelve feet tall. They were regarded as formidable warriors and men of valor (see Gen. 6: 1–6 KJV Holy Bible, *2006 Power Publishing Corp*). The giants were a hybrid race of humans that were the offspring from the sexual union of the "daughters of man" and the "sons of God." "Sons of God" referred to fallen angels who, disrespecting the boundaries set by God, violated their own sexual nature and begat children with the humans. This was an attempt by the devil and his angels to corrupt the messianic lineage through whom the Savior would be born. That is why he targeted "the daughters of man."

The Nephilim created a system of religion that dealt with worshipping idols to glorify the devil. The religion included witchcraft and sorcery, and occult rituals of sexual perversion that contaminated every human who would come under their influence. Thus, many human civilizations and cultures in the time of the Nephlim fell prey to satanic influence and stopped worshipping the true GOD—or at the very least, they mixed in with right worship of the true GOD; human sacrifice and sexual perversion.

Such was the state of things that God repented in His heart for having created people. As a form of judgment, God decided to limit the age of humans to 120 years and sent a flood because 'only evil was in the heart and purpose of man' (see Gen. 6 KJV Holy Bible, *2006 Power Publishing Corp*). Up until that point, the plants were irrigated by mist that used to come up from the ground (Gen. 2:6 KJV Holy Bible, *2006 Power Publishing Corp*), but the ecological system was going to be changed. In exchange, water was going to come from the heavens; this began with the flood. The rain was more abundant and powerful than people had ever seen.

Noah and his family were spared from dying in the flood. He preached for a hundred years while he was building the ark. His fellow countrymen did not believe him; they called him crazy because they had never seen rain come down. They were only used to seeing mist come up. They had never seen a ship like the one Noah was building in the middle of the desert with no body of water surrounding him.

Noah's neighbors were shocked when they saw the rain that did fall, and they became scared. They probably tried to run for safety in the ark, but it was too late. God had closed the door. At that point, the judgment began. Because of his faith, and because there was no contamination with the fallen angels in his generation, Noah was saved. However, the rest of the world's population, including the Nephilim, were obliterated and perished under the water.

With conjecture, it is probable that another flux of fallen angels occurred after the flood, and their mingling with human women begat the giants again. It is alluded to in Sodom and Gomorra that people were perverted and going after "strange flesh" [Jude 1:7 (KJV Holy Bible, *2006 Power Publishing Corp*)]. This refers to the bodies of the incarnate celestial beings.

One of the descendants of the giants was Goliath. According to the Bible, he was about nine feet nine. He was an experienced warrior. For more than a month, he challenged the army of Israel to give him a man to fight, but nobody dared to.

But enter the hero, David, and things turned around. He had come to visit his brothers in the army. He heard the giant's challenge and immediately decided that he wanted to respond to the defiance of the giant. Only an adolescent, David was a little over five feet tall. When he tried to put on the raiment of the soldiers, he couldn't carry it because it was too heavy. By contrast, Goliath was an intimidating warrior, possibly weighing upwards of four hundred pounds. He had a special helmet, and his sword matched his stature. He was extremely confident in his abilities. From a natural perspective, it was highly one-sided fight. There was no physical or natural way that David could defeat the giant.

When King Saul heard about David's intentions, he tried to discourage David, but David wanted to fight Goliath even more. He was sure God was greater than the Philistine—and that he would defeat the giant in the name of Jehovah. When David saw the Israelite army's response to Goliath, he asked them in a tone that displayed his intolerance of the giant's remarks and felt the humiliation that the people of God were being put through. He said, "For who is this uncircumcised Philistine, that he should defy the armies of the living God?" (see 1 Sam. 17:26 KJV Holy Bible, *2006 Power Publishing Corp*). By that point, David was ready to battle the giant.

Most likely, by oral tradition, David had heard about the giants, their religious practices, and what they represented. He knew the kind of enemy he had to fight, but he also knew how much greater God was. He believed the Lord would deliver the giant into his hands.

David had seen the hand of God giving him a supernatural strength. It was the same power that Samson had previously demonstrated against the Philistines. David used this power to fight against the wild lions and bears, and he had been able to kill them to protect his sheep (1 Sam. 17:34 KJV Holy Bible, *2006 Power Publishing Corp*). How much more would he do in order to defend God's name and honor?

In a similar manner, he figured, God could surely enable him to kill the giant. He mentioned it to the king. The king was agreeable and let him fight the giant.

When he finally got ready to meet with the giant, he took his slingshot and five pebbles. The first stone hit the giant on the forehead and made him collapse. According to some physicists and medical doctors, the pebble would have had to travel at a speed of around fifty miles an hour and hit him in the right spot in order to be lethal. When David slung the stone, it wasn't only his strength; God's power was behind it. By his act of faith, the pebble was allowed to travel beyond the natural limitations; it was wrapped up in God's power. No longer was it David's ability; God's power had taken over. David and Jehovah were working as a team to defeat a common enemy.

God's intervention caused David's natural action to become a supernatural action. David caused the giant to fatally collapse, and he took the giant's sword and cut its head off. He killed the giant that day and won a great victory for his nation (see1 Sam. 17:46-58 KJV Holy Bible, *2006 Power Publishing Corp*). His faith brought about the victory. Likewise, you can defeat the giants in your life or in your circumstances if you use your faith.

What is the giant in your life? Is it the giant of debt or finances? Is it the giant of sickness? Is it the giant of a bad habit or an addiction? Is the giant depression or loneliness? Could it be a desire to commit suicide? Perhaps it's a weakness for sexual immorality. Maybe you're ashamed of the fact that you're in jail or have been in the past. Is a bad reputation haunting you wherever you go? Whatever it is, you can have the victory over it now by faith in the name of Jesus. His promises are true, and they are for you. Amen.

Make the following declaration of faith to apply this secret:

> I declare that, by faith, I will receive my miracle. No matter the size of my problem, God is greater than it. I declare that I live by faith and not by sight. Even though my physical eyes may not see it, I believe I have my answer because God is almighty. He is able. He is faithful to his Word, and He loves me. Thank You, Lord, for you have defeated my enemy, the giant of _____.
> Thank You, Lord, and I give you all the glory. Amen.

Secret III

Faith Has Two Kinds of Results: Instantaneous Miracles and Progressive Miracles

Most of the miracles performed by Jesus during His earthly ministry were instantaneous. The gospels are full of them. I offer one particular case as an example of a progressive miracle.

It happened in the town of Bethsaida (see Mark 8:22–26 KJV Holy Bible, *2006 Power Publishing Corp*). The name Bethsaida means "House of Fish." It was a town dedicated to the fishing industry. Life transpired quietly there—except when Jesus visited for the first time. There was a lot of commotion when the throngs were filled with emotion because of the miraculous works of Jesus.

Jesus, the Messiah, (also called Yessuah) and His disciples decided to pay a second visit to preach the gospel, heal the sick, and deliver the oppressed from the devil. On this occasion, the town was alive. There was excitement in the air since they were anticipating the miracles Jesus most likely would perform amongst them.

To begin with, some men got together and brought a blind man before Jesus. They were beseeching Jesus to heal him. We do not know if they brought him because he could not find the place by himself, because he could not see, or because they were concerned for him. At any rate, the blind man represents a person lost in his or her sins who is unable to come to God unless he or she gets help.

In this story, the friends represent the Holy Spirit and the church. The first thing Jesus did was take him outside the village, out of his comfort zone. The purpose was to have the man in total submission to His will and without any hindrances to his faith—from out of the village onto the road to recovery.

It took faith on the part of the blind man to entrust his life to the hands of Jesus. He would trust Jesus' judgment. Wherever He was taking him by the hand, he would be all right. He knew Jesus really cared and wouldn't do him any wrong. Wherever He took him would be safe; Jesus knew better. He abandoned himself to Jesus' leading. Whatever your circumstances, you can trust Jesus—perhaps you need a healing miracle, need Him to restore you morally, need Him to help you save your marriage, or you are in jail unjustly. Do you need a financial miracle or feel lonely because of the loss of a loved one?

Let Him take you by the hand and lead you to the healing place, the place of restoration, the place of provision, the place where you will see His power manifested on your behalf. In his infinite wisdom, He knows precisely what your heart is longing for.

Jesus was going to make it possible for the blind man to be healed and recover his sight, his status, his place in society, his functionality, and his moral integrity.

You and I may not need to recover from blindness, but we need to recover our spiritual sight, our status with God, our place in our relationship with the Father. We need to recover our moral integrity after we are forgiven. That is why God sometimes takes us out of our comfort zones, in order to deal with us, and to have us conform us to His image; His purpose; His character; and His will. He works with us individually as we surrender total control of our lives, in total submission.

Jesus, in a manner rarely seen in His healing ministry, spat in the man's eyes. Then after laying His hands upon him, He asked, "Can you see?" [Mark 8:23 KJV Holy Bible, *2006 Power Publishing Corp*)].

The blind man responded, "I see the men like trees walking." In other words, he was telling Jesus that his vision was not clear; it was blurry, imperfect. Apparently, the blind man had become blind, but this was not his original condition. We infer this because he was able to identify the images—even though they were not perfect.

When Jesus heard the answer, He touched the blind man again. This time around, the blind man was healed from his blindness. He could see totally well; his vision was clear, even at a distance. He could see the expressions of surprise on the faces of the spectators and the friendly smiles of the children who had witnessed his healing. The miracle had been completed. He was no longer blind. He had been restored. Halleluiah!

The narrative shows us that some miracles are progressive or a progression of events. All along, the faith of the receiver of the miracle is being tested. The length of the faith is being tested. Is there any endurance to your faith? Are suffering and patience accompanying your faith? Our answers to those questions determine the outcome of the situation.

When you are confronted with a similar situation in your life, the most productive response is to keep on believing, relying upon, and trusting. The miracle will be completed.

Jesus is the Alpha and the Omega, the beginning and the end. God started the miracle and will bring it to completion. If you trust in Him, He will finish his work. We have seen many cases of this order, and we have seen the hand of the Lord completing the job.

I want you to repeat this declaration of faith to put the lesson into practice.

> I declare that I receive my miracle by faith. I understand that sometimes it may be instantaneous—and sometimes it may be progressive in its manifestation in the physical realm—but I declare it done in the spiritual realm by faith, and I thank God for it. I declare that I know God is at work, and my prayers are being answered because His promises are good.
>
> I believe, according to Luke 11:9, "Ask and it shall be given unto you, knock and it shall be open, seek and you shall find." I have asked; therefore, I receive. I have knocked; therefore, it shall be opened. I have sought; therefore, I shall find. I've received my miracle in the name of Jesus. Amen.

SECRET IV

Faith Has Two Polarities

Faith is similar to Electricity. Electricity is a natural phenomenon; it is harnessed and channeled for constructive use. Electricity is composed of two poles: positive and negative. It is the union of the two currents that produces electricity. It is the same with faith. The positive pole is the belief side, and the negative pole is the disbelief side.

Every portion of faith is composed of the two polarities. The positive polarity, or pole, is the belief part. The polarity of faith that believes God can and will perform a miracle is the supernatural side. It is entirely given to humankind by God when the Word of God is heard. "Faith comes by hearing, hearing from the Word of God" [Rom. 10:17 KJV Holy Bible, *2006 Power Publishing Corp*)].

Faith is a gift given to the human spirit. It is God's contribution to humankind's faith. Like every good thing, it comes from God (see James 1:17 KJV Holy Bible, *2006 Power Publishing Corp*).

The negative polarity is the disbelief side, the doubting side. It is the natural side that doubts the willingness of God. This part believes the human report, the symptoms, the doctor, and the tradition more than the person believes the promise or the Word of God.

The negative polarity of faith believes the symptoms of the sickness more than the Word of God. We can see this explained by the narrative given in Mark 9:14–29 KJV Holy Bible, *2006 Power Publishing Corp.* The case is described in the following manner.

A certain man came looking for Jesus. He came to see Him so Jesus could heal his son. He did not find Him because Jesus was at the Mountain of Transfiguration with the other disciples. Since he could not find Him, the man asked the disciples to pray for his son, but they could not heal him.

In the meantime, Jesus had returned and found the crowd surrounding the man, his son, and the disciples. A deaf and dumb spirit tormented the son; he could not hear or talk. Every now and then, the demon would cause the boy to have seizures and foam at the mouth. The demon acted out right in front of Jesus; he was bold and challenged Jesus because every demon knows who Jesus is.

The man said, "If You can do anything for us, have mercy on us, heal my son."

In other words, Jesus, if you can, if you are capable, and if you are willing: heal my son.

Jesus' answer puts the situation in the right perspective for all those listening to the conversation (and, by extension, you and me). It was not a matter of whether He was capable or willing; the real questions were: Can you believe? Is your faith strong enough to believe that I am capable of healing your son?

The man understood the words of Jesus and immediately replied, "Lord, I believe, help Thou my unbelief" (Mark 9:24, KJV Holy Bible, *2006 Power Publishing Corp*). Some Bible versions say, "Lord, I believe, help my weak faith to become stronger" (New Life Version Bible, 1969 *Christian Literature International*).

As we can see, belief (faith or trust) is accompanied by disbelief (no faith or trust). The positive and negative poles of faith are exposed simultaneously; consequently, greater measures of faith will be accompanied by less measures of disbelief. Until your belief polarity is greater than your disbelief polarity, the miracle will not manifest.

When Jesus heard the father's confession, he immediately proceeded to heal the boy. Thus, they received their miracle in that very hour.

"Faith comes by hearing" Hebrews 11:1 (KJV Holy Bible, *2006 Power Publishing Corp*). "Faith comes to man, like every good thing that comes from God" [James 1:17 (KJV Holy Bible, *2006 Power Publishing Corp.*)]. As we can see from reading these scriptures, FAITH is a gift that comes from the grace of GOD!

It comes when we hear *rhema*. What is *rhema*? In the Greek language of the New Testament, two words refer to the Word of God: *logos* and *rhema*. *Logos* refers to the written word, and *rhema* refers to the revealed Word of God, the one that is quickened in the heart of the believer when the written Word of God is heard.

The proclamation of the Word of God (*logos*) engenders faith in the heart of the believer. And faith helps the believer perceive the *rhema*, which is the revelation of what God is going to do. When the "*logos*" meets the "*rhema*", they become unified. The Word of God generates faith. The "*logos*" hovers over the "*rhema*", and the miracle is conceived in the spirit of the believer. The *rhema* (the revelation) is given at the moment the Word (*logos*) is spoken. After this, it becomes a seed that is implanted in the hearts, or spirits, of people. It then germinates and bears fruit according to the kind of soil. It may give the harvest of 30, or 60 or 100 percent (see Mark 4 KJV Holy Bible, *2006 Power Publishing Corp*).

What kind of soil are you?

Let us be fertile ground for the Lord. Let your life produce many fruits of faith for His glory. Let the *logos* and the *rhema* function jointly in your spirit by faith. Let them produce the miracle you need in your life.

To apply the lesson, I want you to make the following declaration of faith in a loud voice:

> I declare that I will believe with all my heart. I will not allow doubt to rob me of my faith. I renounce to all doubting in my heart or spirit. I cast down all doubt and subdue it to my faith … according to the revelation I have received. I understand that in order for me to receive my miracle, my belief has to be greater, stronger, than my disbelief. I can surely say, "Lord I believe, help my disbelief" so I can receive your answer. Amen.

SECRET V

The Milestones of Faith

The first milestone of faith is the *inception*. This happens when the *rhema* (the revelation of the miracle of what God is going to perform as promised by the written word, *logos*) is given to "the believer." Faith to receive the miracle is then implanted in the human spirit. This is the moment of inception, the first milestone.

The inception takes place when the Word of God impregnates the spirit. The moment of inception happens as an act of God, by which the human spirit is invited to receive the impregnation of the promise as proclaimed in the Word of God. Then, you receive the revelation (*rhema*) of what God wants to do.

The second milestone is *conception*. This takes place as the miracle is forming and organizing itself in the human spirit. It is growing like the embryo grows in the womb; like the embryo, it needs to be nourished, fed, taken care of by the reading of the Word, maintaining an atmosphere of faith, continuing to worship, etc. As the miracle is growing in your spirit, continue praising Him and continue to give Him thanks in advance for what He is doing and what will manifest.

Delivery is the third milestone. This takes place when the miracle is born, when the miracle is made manifest for the natural world to see what happened in the spiritual or supernatural realm. A miracle case that illustrates the sequence of these milestones is the healing of the woman with an issue of blood (see Mark 5 KJV Holy Bible, *2006 Power Publishing Corp*).

A middle-class woman approached Jesus for a miracle. She apparently had owned a house and had a husband, but he left her when she became ill. She probably did not have any kids because of her sickness. She had been sick for twelve long years.

She was sick with a blood issue. She probably had to sell her house and her furniture to invest in her health. She had paid the best physicians of the country to procure a cure. She spent all she had, and her situation was worse than before. Poor and with no hope, her only chance at salvation was Jesus.

Watch this carefully. "When she heard the report concerning Jesus", she received the revelation, the *rhema*, of her healing. That is when the milestone of inception occurred. The promise of healing was impregnated into her spirit (see Mark 5:27 KJV Holy Bible, *2006 Power Publishing Corp*).

She pushed herself through the throngs and said, "If I only could touch His garment, I will be healed." She was repeating this to herself constantly. Without knowing, she was conceiving her miracle. She was going through the milestone of conception (see Mark 5:28 KJV Holy Bible, *2006 Power Publishing Corp*).

After she touched the Lord's garment, the source of her blood issue was immediately healed (see Mark 5:29 KJV Holy Bible, *2006 Power Publishing Corp*). The milestone of delivery had taken place. The miracle happened, and Jesus asked, "Who touched me?"

The disciples said, "You see the throngs of people touching you, and you asked who has touched you?"

Jesus replied, "I know somebody touched me because power came out of me." The woman with the blood issue had so much faith that touching the Lord's garment withdrew power from Him.

Part of the healing anointing that was deposited into Jesus was transferred to her, and she was instantly healed. Jesus had recognized this moment and openly confessed that power had come out of Him. Regardless of the hopelessness of her situation, the impossibility of the crowds blocking her way—and not taking into account the criticisms of the people or considering the weakness of her body—she knew touching Jesus would heal her. Great was her faith. She went through the process of the milestones of faith and obtained her miracle.

I want you to know that there were a lot of witnesses to this miracle; a throng was following Jesus, but she was the only recipient of the miracle. She was healed and restored that very same hour. Her testimony has transcended time and history; she will forever be remembered as a woman who believed in God and received her miracle.

What milestone or moment of the miracle are you in? Keep believing, trusting, and relying on the Lord.

He will show up; He will come to His appointment, and everything is going to be all right. Keep believing until the delivery of your miracle occurs. You will see the glory of God just like the woman with the blood issue. Amen.

Putting the lesson into practice, I want you to repeat in a loud voice:

> I declare that I am willing and ready to receive God's Word concerning my miracle. I will abide by His Word and believe that God will help me through the process of inception and conception even to the time of delivery of my miracle. I believe my miracle will soon be manifested in the physical realm, and I will give Him praise and glory in Jesus' name. Amen.

SECRET VI

Faith Knows No Boundaries

Capernaum was a very active city; the name means "village of comfort" (Luke 7:1–10). It was located in the northwestern part of the Sea of Galilee. Jesus used it as the home for His ministry in Galilee. The disciples Peter, Andrew, and Matthew were originally from there.

Jesus performed many miracles there, including bringing Jairus' daughter back to life and healing Peter's mother-in-law.

Once when Jesus came to Capernaum, a certain centurion approached Jesus and told Him his servant was sick and about to die. He wanted Jesus to heal him. The people who surrounded the man told Jesus that he was worthy of the miracle because he had built a synagogue for them. Jesus was aware of this because he had taught in the synagogue several times.

The centurion was professionally committed to the Roman Caesar, but spiritually, he was committed to the God of Israel. That was why he had had built the synagogue at Capernaum for the Jewish people to worship. He believed in Jehovah, and he believed Jesus was the Messiah (Luke 7:1–5 KJV Holy Bible, *2006 Power Publishing Corp*).

The centurion had heard so much about Jesus. The sickness of his servant provided the opportunity for him to meet Jesus. Reflecting upon his own request, he changed his mind about it. He said, 'I am a man under authority. I tell my servants to come, and they come. To others, I say go—and they go. You do not have to come to my house, but just say the Word, and my servant will be healed' [Mark 7:7,8 (KJV Holy Bible, *2006 Power Publishing Corp*)].

Jesus replied, "I have not seen such faith, not even in Israel" (see Mark 7:9 KJV Holy Bible, *2006 Power Publishing Corp*).

The centurion found out later that his servant had been healed from the hour Jesus said, "Go, and according to your faith, it shall be done" KJV Holy Bible, *2006 Power Publishing Corp*).

Faith knows no boundaries. The centurion received a revelation (*rhema*) by his faith. He knew he was with Jesus. He was "here," and he knew his servant was "there" at his house. Nevertheless, he said, "Say the Word, and my servant shall be healed." He knew that faith knows no distance and has no boundaries. As soon as he initiated his return, his other servants came to tell him that the young servant had been healed. Regardless of the distance, the miracle took place.

Certainly, faith knows no distance. What happened to him could happen to you. God is no respecter of persons. He doesn't discriminate. What He did for others, He could do for you. When He looks at you, all that He desires to see is your faith. When you are asking for a miracle for you, you're loved ones, or somebody you know, remember that faith knows no boundaries.

It still works the same way. You can be wherever you are right now, and the people that you pray for could be in China or anywhere else. If you have faith, your prayer will be answered, and the miracle will happen even at a distance. I encourage you to pray for them. God will work in their lives because faith has no boundaries.

Another example is the healing of the daughter of the Gentile woman (Matt. 15). Jesus was going on His evangelistic tour of the area of Tyre and Sidon. Prior to this, Jesus had been in Jerusalem. Jesus sat down, and a crowd began to gather around Him. People were diseased, blind, deaf, mute, paralyzed, and maimed. Some had Parkinson's and other nervous diseases. The multitude asked Him to allow them to touch His garment so they could be healed.

The anointing that was upon Jesus had permeated even His garment. The crowd found that out, and that is why they asked Him to let them touch it. This stems from the case of the woman with the blood issue. The Bible says, 'All of them that touched Him got healed' Matthew 15: 29-31 (see KJV Holy Bible, *2006 Power Publishing Corp*). Even the people without arms or hands received creative miracles, and their arms and legs began growing back instantly. Soon after, Jesus departed to the region of Tyre and Sidon.

This area was predominantly populated by Gentiles; the Israelites were the minority. The Israelites used to refer to this ethnic group maliciously as the "seed of dogs." The

Gentiles were aware of this demeaning connotation. Their culture had gotten them used to it, and they tolerated it. A woman in the area had a desperate need. She had a beautiful daughter, but she was possessed and tormented by a satanic entity. She heard rumors that Jesus was coming to town and decided her daughter's situation was so bad that only God's intervention could turn things around. Perhaps you are in a similar situation.

Whatever your problem, you know that only God's intervention in your life can change things around. You have come to the point where you desperately need God. This Gentile woman felt that it was necessary to go meet Jesus. She must have thought, *He is coming to my town, and I am not going to miss this opportunity.*

So, equipped with her faith and propelled by her need, she decided to walk the dusty roads of her town and travel on a journey of faith to encounter Jesus. She knew she was heading in the right direction. You are too if you have decided to seek God in the midst of your problem.

She came as close to Jesus as the crowd permitted her to and began to cry at the top of her lungs, 'Have mercy on me, O Lord, Son of David. My daughter is severely demon possessed' Matthew 15: 21-319 (see KJV Holy Bible, *2006 Power Publishing Corp*). She had heard enough testimonies from other Israelites to know that He was the Messiah sent from God. That's why she addressed Him as "Lord, Son of David." She was confessing, through her cry, that she believed in Him. But Jesus did not say a word. Jesus' silence was an opportunity for her to reexamine her heart. Did she have the right motive for her request? Did she have enough faith? Jesus was testing her faith.

Even Jesus, in a moment of intense suffering on the cross as a true human being, felt the silence of God when He was carrying the sins of the world. Jesus felt as if the Father had abandoned Him, and He said, "Father, why have thou forsaken me?"

The Father was testing Jesus' faith. This was the supreme test. Did He believe the Father would accept His sacrifice? Did He have faith that He would have a large family of believers following Him after He was resurrected from the dead? Did He believe that He would be given all authority in heaven and on earth? Did He believe that miracles and wonders would be performed in His name? Did He believe the Holy Spirit had the power to raise Him from the dead? Obviously He passed the test; Jesus is the "author and finisher of our faith" (see Hebrews 12:2 KJV Holy Bible, *2006 Power Publishing Corp*).How could He have required us to have faith if He did not have any Himself?

Have you ever been there? Have you wondered why you pray to God but feel like He isn't answering you? He seems to be absent or deaf. He simply does not answer. You might ask, "Where are You, God?" Has He rejected you? Does He care about you? "Why have you forsaken me?"

Take heart, my friend. He heard you before you even opened your mouth. He cares for you; He is simply testing your faith. He has promised He will not leave you or forsake you. God loves you, and He loves to answer your prayers.

The Gentile woman, taking control of all her emotions, doubts, and questions, decided to resist doubting. She continued to cry out and be persistent until she got an answer. She was not going to give up. She didn't care about her critics or the opinion of the crowd. She was not going to consider the criticism of the disciples either. They told the Lord to 'dismiss her because she is crying behind us, and she is annoying to us' Matthew 15:23 (see KJV Holy Bible, *2006 Power Publishing Corp*).Yes, my friend, sometimes even the church or disciples will criticize us when we do not get answers. When this happens, keep believing, continue with your faith, and continue asking. Disregard the critics.

Jesus answered, "I was not sent, except to the lost sheep of the house of Israel." His priority was the Israelites, and she was a Gentile. He did not have to answer her request.

She would not give up. She escalated her request, saying, "Lord, help me."

Jesus said, "It is no good to take the children's bread and throw it to the little dogs."

She replied, "Yes, Lord, yet even the little dogs eat the crumbs which fall from the master's table." In other words, she was acknowledging that she wasn't an Israelite, yet she believed that even a bit of the overflow of the blessing pertaining to the Israelites would take care of her needs.

As you can see, she was still persistent in her faith, and Jesus agreed to grant her request. Her faith had passed the test. Jesus said, "O woman, great is your faith. Let it be to you as you desire."

Her faith was bigger than all the obstacles, objections, denials, theological reasons, and doubts. Her persistent faith triumphed over all, and she got the results she wanted. Her daughter was healed from that very hour

(Matt. 15:28 KJV Holy Bible, *2006 Power Publishing Corp*).

Her daughter was not even there. She was at home, some distance away in the area of Tyre and Sidon. It was enough that she was talking to the Almighty Lord; she believed that Jesus' authorization would be sufficient for the miracle to happen. Since faith has no boundaries, the distance did not matter.

God is no respecter of persons. He does not discriminate. If you have faith, He will do the same for you.

To put the lesson into practice, I want you to repeat the following declaration of faith:

> I declare that my prayers are answered when I pray for someone, even if he or she is in a different physical place, even at a distance. God will intervene, and the miracle will occur because my faith has no boundaries, and it will work the same. Amen.

SECRET VII

Faith Adapts Itself to the Need

No miracle request is too small or too big. Faith meets all demands. It is like a towel that adapts itself to the size of the hands or feet. A towel is a towel, and it will accommodate anybody and everybody.

Whether you need a healing miracle, a financial miracle, a provision miracle, or even a lifesaving miracle, faith is necessary for everything.

"Without faith, it is impossible to please God" (Heb. 11:6 KJV Holy Bible, *2006 Power Publishing Corp.*).

How was the woman with the blood issue healed? She was healed by faith (Mark 5:28 KJV Holy Bible, *2006 Power Publishing Corp*).

How was the centurion's servant healed? The servant was healed by faith (Luke 7:1–10 KJV Holy Bible, *2006 Power Publishing Corp*).

How was the Red Sea divided? It was divided by faith (Ex.14 KJV Holy Bible, *2006 Power Publishing Corp*).

There are many more miracles that we cannot mention due to a lack of time, but we will consider one more (Acts

5:17–21 KJV Holy Bible, *2006 Power Publishing Corp*). The protagonists were Peter and John; of course, the other disciples were there too.

Soon after Jesus' ascension into heaven, the church started preaching the gospel and fulfilling the Great Commission. Peter and John healed a lame man. The scribes and the Sadducees were greatly disturbed on the account of them preaching and performing miracles in the name of Jesus. They became upset and threw them both in jail for the evening.

The next day, the apostles went back to preaching again. This time, they were forbidden to preach the name of Jesus. The apostles responded by praying to God. They said, "Now, Lord, look on their threats and grant to your servants that with all boldness, they may speak Your Word by stretching out your hand to heal in the signs, and wonders may be done in the name of Your Holy Servant Jesus." It was a prayer asking for boldness to preach.

The Bible says that when they prayed, the place where they were assembled was shaken. They were all filled with the Holy Spirit. They spoke the Word of God with boldness. Soon after, the high priest —who was filled with indignation—put Peter and John in a common prison, see Acts. 5: (KJV Holy Bible, *2006 Power Publishing Corp*).

At night, an angel of the Lord opened the prison doors and brought them out, saying, "Go and stand in the temple and speak to the people, all the words of this life." The angel opened the door to the prison and blinded the prison guards so they couldn't see what was happening. They took out Peter and John and put them in the street, free to go. The angel came back and locked the door again.

The next morning, Peter and John went back to preaching. Talk about boldness! Peter and John had it, especially after experiencing the deliverance performed by the angel where they were supernaturally set free. Their prayers had been answered miraculously by faith. Faith adapted itself to their needs. They prayed for boldness with the same faith that led to the lame man being healed.

So my friend, trust in the Lord—your answer may be on the way.

The rest of these stories that weren't mentioned were all brought about by faith.

According to your faith, it shall be done.

If you need a financial miracle, you cannot buy it. All you need is faith.

If you need a healing miracle, all you need is faith.

If you need salvation, all you need is faith.

If you want God to bring back your husband or your wife, all you need is faith.

If you want God to have your son or daughter or someone else delivered from a habit, all you need is faith. The common denominator to all miracles is faith. The same kind of faith is the prerequisite of all miracles. Use your faith to receive any and all the miracles you need in your life.

Now declare in a loud voice to exercise the lesson learned in this chapter:

> I declare, and I believe, the Word of God. It tells me that the only way to please God is by faith, and He rewards those who diligently seek Him. I am approaching Him by faith.

I believe He is rewarding me by granting me the miracle I am asking from Him. By faith, I declare that I receive my miracle pertaining to (fill in the blank with your request) in the name of Jesus. Amen.

Secret VIII

Faith: Once it's Yours, Nobody Can Use It but You

Faith transitions from God's possession to people's possessions.

Faith transitions from God to people. "The Word was with God" [John 1:1 (KJV Holy Bible, *2006 Power Publishing Corp)*]. The promises of God for humankind were with Him. They were under His possession.

But lo and behold, enter a pleading, crying child of His into the picture. The child claims the promise and faith and transitions from His possession into the possession of the believer. It is no longer His; it is the believer's. Faith becomes the possession of the miracle-seeking person!

Let's look at some examples.

There was a woman in Magdala. She was a sister to Lazarus. Apparently she had lived a very promiscuous life. She ended up enslaved to Satan and was possessed by demons. She had seven demons that used to torment her. She was brought before Jesus for deliverance. Jesus—with his uncommon love and compassion—ministered to her even though she was morally indignant. Jesus saw her as a woman of great potential if she were restored. He knew that once transformed and delivered, she could become an asset for his cause. Jesus set her free. The demons were gone, her mind was sound, and she was in control and back to normal.

Jesus concluded his ministering to Mary Magdalene by saying, "Thy faith has saved you, go in peace" [Luke 7:50 (KJV Holy Bible, *2006 Power Publishing Corp)*]. Mary Magdalene became a staunch follower of Jesus. She ministered to the Lord with her own finances. She was dedicated to promoting his ministry.

When Jesus was about to be crucified, she decided to break an alabaster flask and anoint His head and feet. She used her hair to wipe His feet. Jesus called attention to this act of worship and said that she would be remembered forever as the woman who anointed Jesus' head and feet in preparation for His burial wherever this gospel would be preached.

She was greatly criticized by the disciples, especially by Judas. They all saw it as a waste of money. The perfume was very expensive; its value compared to a year's wages. It was the disciples' opinion that the perfume could have been sold and the money given to the poor.

Jesus replied, "You will always have the poor with you, but you won't always have me."

Her faith caused her to be delivered from the demonic oppression, and her promiscuous life ended. She became a totally new person. Her faith had made her well [Mark 14: 3-9 (KJV Holy Bible, *2006 Power Publishing Corp)*].

A blind man was sitting by the road in Jericho. It was a reconstruction of the Jericho in the Old Testament, which had been the scenario of a great miracle.

The people of God had marched around the wall for seven days. The walls of the city were thick enough to carry several chariots and horses. Inside the walls, there was a space big enough to operate an inn and some other living quarters. Rahab was a harlot who owned an inn there. That's where she hid the Israelite spies when they came to scout the city prior to the conquest.

The march was to be done once a day, except for the seventh day; on that day, they had to march around the town seven times. At that same time, they were blowing their trumpets. The people of Israel completed the instructions given by God. The strong walls of Jericho collapsed from the bottom, and the people of Israel saw that the defenseless city was accessible and ready for possession. Their faith had operated a miracle. The walls fell down, and Israel conquered Jericho—just as God had promised. Their faith had brought about their victory.

My friend, if you trust in the Lord, the walls that protect the Jericho of your life will fall—and you will take possession of whatever miracle you are expecting from God.

Going back to our story, the blind man heard a crowd passing by. He asked what this meant. He wanted to know why they were screaming and behaving tumultuously. They told him that Jesus of Nazareth was passing by. Immediately, he saw the opportunity of a lifetime. This was the big break he was waiting for. He could receive his sight and be restored, if only Jesus could hear him.

He began to cry out, saying, "Jesus, Son of David, have mercy on me."

Jesus stood still and commanded him to be brought to Him.

He came to Jesus, crying and saying, "Son of David, have mercy on me."

Jesus said, "What do you want ME to do for you?"

The blind man of Jericho said, "Lord, that I may receive my sight."

Jesus said, "Receive your sight. Your faith has made you whole."

After Jesus tested the man's faith and found that it was strong, he granted him the miracle. Jesus said, "Your faith has made you well."

Jesus recognized that his faith had brought about the miracle. Do you have faith? Is it strong and powerful enough to produce a miracle? If the answer is yes, then you have taken possession of the promise. Now, it is *your faith*—and nobody else can use it. *You* are equipped to supernaturally conquer the impossible [Luke18: 35-39 (KJV Holy Bible, *2006 Power Publishing Corp)*]. "For with God nothing shall be impossible": [Luke 1:37 (KJV Holy Bible, *2006 Power Publishing Corp)*].

Summarizing the lesson, we have established that the miracle will not happen until <u>*somebody*</u> appropriates the promise. How about you? You can be that somebody. Are you ready to appropriate God's promise? If you are ready to say that God's promises are yours, get ready for the miracle.

"<u>Thy faith</u>" is a wonderful phrase because it means that nobody can take it away from you or steal it from you.

"Thy faith" is waiting for you to use it. There is a miracle coming your way—if you only believe.

Go ahead, my friend, use your faith; it is rightfully yours. If you—or any loved ones— need a healing, use your faith and receive your miracle.

If you need a job, claim it and receive it. If you need your husband or wife to come home to you, use your faith to bring him or her home. If your daughter or son is lost in drug addiction, alcohol, or any other bad habit, use your faith to see her or him change. Whatever your need is, exercise your faith and receive your miracle.

I want you to repeat this declaration of faith:

> I declare that I am willing and ready to use my faith. I understand that nobody can use my faith but me. Putting my faith in action, I declare that I receive my miracle. God has answered my request. I needed God to (fill in the blank with your petition). By faith, I declare it done. I will give testimony of what God has done for me. Praise the Lord. Amen.

Secret IX

Miracles May Take Time to Manifest

Between believing the promise and the actual materialization or manifestation of the promise, a lapse of time may occur. It may be one minute or twenty years or four thousand years. Such as the time it took from the promise given to Adam and Eve in paradise when God pronounced the curse upon the serpent: *examine Gen. 3:15* (KJV Holy Bible, *2006 Power Publishing Corp).*

It took a simple, believing woman to accept the motherhood of the Savior when the time was right. Then it happened. The manifestation took place. It happened at the time appointed in God's calendar, in His time. Have you considered the time factor for why your miracle has not been manifested? Have you given a chance to God's calendar?

Do not make the mistake that Sarah and Abraham made. It all began when God appeared unto Abraham and told him He would bless him with numerous descendants and that he would be the father of many nations. Abraham believed God, but he was childless because his wife was sterile.

They wanted to see the child God had promised them, and they tried to help God. Sarah came up with the idea of being the first surrogate mother in the history of the Bible. It seemed to be a brilliant idea to her at the time. Why not allow Abraham to be with her maid? Hagar could conceive a child, which according to the custom of the time, would be considered born of Sara. Thus, they did not have to wait, and God's promise to them would be fulfilled. But wait and see what happens.

Ishmael was born, and Abraham loved him dearly. Hagar began to mistreat Sara and acted with despondency toward her because she'd had Abraham's child—and Sarah was sterile. She thought she had the right to have Abraham prefer her as his wife. Talk about taking over. But Sarah proved her wrong and eventually evicted her from her house with Abraham's approval. The family was divided; there was a lot of strife and heartache. This is evident today when you look at the way Arab nations (children of Ishmael) and the Israelites (children of Jacob, descendants of Isaac) treat each other. It was a bad idea to try to help God.

They were terribly wrong in trying to precipitate the fulfillment of the promise. My friend, God does not need help; he is an Almighty God and can perform a miracle in spite of all human impossibilities. He will do it in his time—and according to His infinite wisdom. Just let go—and let God be God. Allow Him to answer you at the appointed time. Amen.

Some other factors may delay the manifestation of a miracle. Sometimes, faith needs to be stronger. This was the case of the people of Israel; instead of taking possession of the Promised Land in two weeks, they went around in circles for forty years because they lacked faith. They had seen God send the ten plagues to the Egyptians and how Pharaoh, incapable of any further resistance, had to let them go free from slavery.

They had seen the supernatural guidance from a cloud during the day, which would also protect them from the blazing desert sun. At night, he used a pillar of fire to provide them with light and heat, to guide them through the desert, and to protect them from extremely cold weather (see Ex. 13: KJV Holy Bible, *2006 Power Publishing Corp).* They had seen God divide the Red Sea, and they could cross on dry land (see Ex. 14: KJV Holy Bible, *2006 Power Publishing Corp).*They saw Pharaoh and his chariots perish when he attempted to take them back into slavery.

When they had no water to drink, they had seen the bitter waters of Mara changed into potable water (see Ex. 15: KJV Holy Bible, *2006 Power Publishing Corp).*They had been fed with the daily bread of Manna in the desert (see Ex. 16: KJV Holy Bible, *2006 Power Publishing Corp).* Manna is equivalent to an angel's bread manufactured in heaven. Somehow they could not believe that God could give them the victory over the giants of the land and their fortified cities. Only Joshua and Caleb believed, and they took possession of their portion of the blessing, the miracle of the Promised Land.

The rest of the generation, people older than twenty, died without occupying the territory that God had promised to them. Their doubt and unbelief disallowed them from receiving the Promised Land (see Num. 14: KJV Holy Bible, *2006 Power Publishing Corp*). The weakness of faith prohibited that generation from possessing the land. Do not let your doubts or your lack of faith delay the manifestation of your miracle. Maintain yourself strong in faith like Abraham; he never staggered, wavered, or doubted in his faith. Not considering his own body or the sterility of Sarah, he remained strong in faith by giving glory to God [Rom. 4:20 (KJV Holy Bible, *2006 Power Publishing Corp)*].

Another reason for delays is when we look at circumstances more than we look at God and His power. When we behave as such, we lose focus and perspective; this inhibits us from taking hold of the miracles.

It happened to Peter when Jesus calmed a big storm. Jesus was walking on the water, and Peter asked permission to do the same. At the beginning, Peter was able to walk, but as soon as he began to look at the depth of the water, Peter began to sink. When he asked Jesus to save him, Jesus proceeded to reach down and save him (see Matt. 14:26–33 KJV Holy Bible, *2006 Power Publishing Corp)*.

If you want to receive your miracle, keep your focus. Do not get distracted. Keep your perspective.

Sometimes we talk ourselves out of the miracle by making the wrong confessions and speaking negative words (see Prov. 18:20–21 (KJV Holy Bible, *2006 Power Publishing Corp)*. We do not receive miracles until we correct our confessions. Watch your language. What you say is what you get.

Another major block to receiving manifestation of miracles is un-forgiveness. God demands that we forgive:

'For if ye forgive men their trespasses, your Heavenly Father will also forgive you. But if ye forgive not men their trespasses, neither will your Father forgive your trespasses' (Matt. 6:14–15 KJV Holy Bible, *2006 Power Publishing Corp*). God's forgiveness to us is in direct proportion to our forgiveness to others.

"And when ye stand praying, forgive if ye have aught against any, that your Father also which is in heaven may forgive you your trespasses. But if ye do not forgive, neither will your Father which is in heaven forgive your trespasses" [Mark 11:25–26 (KJV Holy Bible, *2006 Power Publishing Corp*)]. <u>When you pray for a miracle, you ought to forgive your brothers and sisters of their offenses in order to receive your answer.</u>

Give me a minute to walk with you through the innermost chambers of your heart. Come along with me; can you see a jail there? Only you have the key to open the cell door. Who do you see imprisoned? Is it your father? Is it your mother? Is it a distant relative? Is it a close friend? You recognize them because they brought pain into your life. They hurt you. Perhaps they violated your rights. They could have robbed you or exploited you. They could have deceived you. Perhaps they raped you or committed another act of violence against you. They could have caused you pain; for that reason, you hold them prisoner. Now, forgiveness is an act of will. You must choose to let them go free.

Every offense against you is accompanied by pain. Therefore, you must let the pain that came along with your offense go away. You will disempower the force of the aggression or the offense when you let the pain go. Are you ready to forgive?

I want you to do the following: Whatever the name of your prisoner, tell them in a loud voice: _____, I forgive the offense you afflicted upon me. I let you go free. I will not carry the burden anymore. I destroy the pain of the offense, and I order it out of my spirit. Let the blood of Jesus cover them—and let the love of Jesus replace the pain.

The forgiveness is applicable to the offender—and to the offended. The most difficult part comes after you forgive your transgressor. Forgive yourself for having allowed the transgression to hurt you and for permitting it to be such a burden in your life. Forgive yourself, and let the blood of Jesus cover it. Today is a new beginning—without the burden of having the prisoner locked away in the jail cell of your heart. All things have passed away, and everything is made new. Once you give up the past pain, it can no longer control you! You are free to forgive yourself!

<u>Another reason for experiencing a delay in the answering of your miracle is feeling guilt or shame</u>, twin sisters that show up together. Whether real or surreal, fact or imaginary, guilt and shame can block you from receiving your blessing. I know you have committed sins just as everyone else has. I know you haven't had the best behavior, and I know that produces guilt. Shame comes along with the guilt—and is the emotion of unworthiness and sinfulness.

If you have confessed your sins to God, truly feel sorry for your actions, have repented to God, and pleaded the blood of Jesus over it, you are forgiven. There should be no more guilt because your sin is blotted out. There should be no more shame because there's nothing to be ashamed of. Don't let feelings of inferiority, unworthiness, guilt, or shame deprive you of your "*spiritual inheritance*". The blood of Jesus will never lose its power. It has the power to eradicate all the malignant consequences of sin in your life. Forgetting guilt and shame guarantees that you will get your miracle. Get ready, my friend. The miracle is on its way.

I want you to repeat this declaration of faith in a loud voice:

> Now, when the time is right, even though I receive it by faith now, my miracle will happen. It will be manifested in the natural realm. I will let no doubt, wrong confession, or sin delay the manifestation of my miracle. Not before, not after, but when the time is right. When I have totally aligned my words with the Word of God, when my faith is stronger than my doubts, when I stop looking at the circumstances and start looking at God, my miracle will be manifested. Amen.

SECRET X

Faith Requires Planting a Seed

Some people do not get an answer from God—even though they claim to have a lot of faith. Let me introduce you to another secret of faith. These people are never going to harvest a miracle because they have not planted a seed for it.

In order to have a harvest, you must plant a seed. This applies to the natural world as well as the spiritual world. This a principle established by the Almighty God. "While the earth remains, seedtime and harvest, cold and heat, winter and summer, and day and night shall not cease" [Gen. 8:22 (KJV Holy Bible, *2006 Power Publishing Corp)*]. The earth is still remaining, rotating on its axis. The law of gravity is still in effect. The seasons are still succeeding each other in an endless procession. The day is still divided by the night. Therefore, the law or principle of seedtime and harvest is still in effect.

"Be not deceived; God is not mocked: for whatever a man soweth, that shall he also reap" [Galatians 6:7 (KJV Holy Bible, *2006 Power Publishing Corp).*]

Every seed comes with its own set of instructions that are determined by its DNA. The apple seed will produce only apples. The watermelon seed will produce watermelons. The orange seed will produce oranges. Likewise, in the spiritual realm, the seed of bad thoughts will produce bad actions [Luke 6:45 (KJV Holy Bible, *2006 Power Publishing Corp)*]. The seed of generosity will harvest generosity from God.

'For out of the heart proceed evil thoughts, murders, adulteries, fornications, thefts, false witness, and blasphemies' (see Matt.15:19 KJV Holy Bible, *2006 Power Publishing Corp).*

'For from within, out of the heart of men, proceed evil thoughts, adulteries, fornications, murders, thefts, covetousness, wickedness, deceit, lasciviousness, an evil eye, blasphemy, pride, foolishness' (see Mark 7:21–22 KJV Holy Bible, *2006 Power Publishing Corp).*

As you see, evil thoughts are seeds for the harvest of murder, adultery, etc. On the other hand, good thoughts are seeds for a good harvest, according to its own kind. "Honor the Lord with thy substance (possessions) and with the first-fruits of all thine increase so shall thy barns be filled with plenty, and thy presses shall burst out with new wine" [Prov. 3:9–10 (KJV Holy Bible, *2006 Power Publishing Corp)*].

"One thing thou lackest: Go thy way, sell whatsoever thou hast and give to the poor, and thou shalt have treasure in heaven; and come, take up the cross, and follow me" [Mark 10:21 (KJV Holy Bible, *2006 Power Publishing Corp)*].

"Give (plant a seed), and it shall be given unto you (your harvest): good measure, pressed down and shaken together and running over, shall men give into your bosom: 'for with the same measure that ye mete (your seed), therewith it shall be measured to you again", [Luke 6:38 (KJV Holy Bible, *2006 Power Publishing Corp)*].

"He that despiseth his neighbor sinneth, but he that hath mercy on the poor, happy is he" [Prov. 14:21 (KJV Holy Bible, *2006 Power Publishing Corp)*].

"A good man sheweth favor and lendeth; he will guide his affairs with discretion" [Ps. 112:5(KJV Holy Bible, *2006 Power Publishing Corp)*].

> And Jesus sat opposite the treasury, and beheld how the people cast money into the treasury. And many who were rich cast in much. And there came a certain poor widow, and she threw in two mites, which make a farthing. And Jesus called unto Him his disciples and said unto them, "Verily I say unto you, that this poor widow hath cast more in than all they that have cast into the treasury; for they all cast in of their abundance, but she of her want cast in all that she had, even all her living": (see Mark 12:41–44 KJV Holy Bible, *2006 Power Publishing Corp)*.

These verses clarify the fact that it is not only the amount that you give—but also the *proportion* in relation to your resources. If you are a millionaire and give one thousand dollars out of your abundance, it is less in proportion to the offering given by somebody with limited resources—even though it may be a lesser amount. It is worthy to observe that Jesus looks at the offerings of the widow as well as the offerings that you give.

Since God wanted a family on earth, He sent His Son. Those who believe in Jesus become God's family. His Son is the seed, and His family is the harvest. We see biblical examples about sowing seeds. The centurion planted a seed, built a synagogue, and harvested a miracle (the healing of his servant) (see Matt. 8:5–13 KJV Holy Bible, *2006 Power Publishing Corp*).

The widow of Zarephath fed the prophet first as had been instructed by the Lord. She planted a seed, and she received this miracle: her oil and flour multiplied daily, miraculously, and she survived three and a half years of famine (see I Kings 17:8–16 KJV Holy Bible, *2006 Power Publishing Corp*).

The patriarchs of the Old Testament, the kings and heroes, all knew the importance of this principle. They planted seeds in order to get harvests. The Bible is full of promises for those who give. 'Give and it shall be given unto you'. 'He who plants sparingly so will he also reap'. If your prayers are not being answered, and if believing is not enough, give a chance to giving.

The time has come to plant a seed. The Holy Spirit will give you insight into what kind of seed to plant. Before you do anything, pray that God will show you what He wants you to do.

- Give some of your money to help the poor, the needy, and the homeless. Find a charitable organization and become a contributor. Find a church and give your tithes.
- Give an offering to Trinity Broadcasting Corporation or any other evangelistic corporation for the preaching of the gospel.

God likes that. Go ahead and plant a seed. Can you guess what will happen? The miracle will happen! You will receive your miracle. The Lord of the harvest has one for you, and it has your name on it. To put your faith into practice, make the following declaration in a loud voice:

> I declare that, as an expression of my faith, I will plant a seed wherever the Lord wants me to. I know God will honor my faith and will give a harvest to my seed. My seed is leaving my hands—but not my life. I claim that it will come back to me in my future, multiplied and in abundance through the miracles God will perform in my life. Praise the Lord. Amen.

Faith Works with Confession

In the Bible, *confess* means to stand alongside God, to agree with Him, and to declare the same things He declares. If He says you are healed, you are healed. If He says you are righteous, you are righteous. If He says you are forgiven, you are forgiven. If He says you are saved, you are saved. If He says He is your provider, He is your provider. If He says He is your healer, then He is your healer. If He says He will never leave you or forsake you, then He never will leave you or forsake you. Praise God.

By confessing the promises of God, the believer allows his or her faith to become productive. He is allowing his or her faith to work. Faith works with confession.

Faith comes with a creative source of power that is activated when the Word of Faith (the miracle you are asking for) is pronounced. 'The Word of Faith (the miracle you are waiting for or expecting to receive) is near you, even in thy mouth'(see Rom. 10:8 KJV Holy Bible, *2006 Power Publishing Corp).*

When the believer pronounces the miracle he or she needs, something happens in the spiritual realm. The results are seen in the physical realm: that is why the centurion said, "Say or speak the Word, and my servant shall be healed" [Matt. 8 (KJV Holy Bible, *2006 Power Publishing Corp)*].

This explains why Jesus spoke to the storm, and it calmed down and obeyed Him. The disciples said, "What kind of man is this that even the storm and the winds obey Him?"

Jesus said, "If you have faith, you shall speak to the mountain, and the mountain shall move."

What kind of mountain is in your life? Is it a sickness or a failed relationship? Is it financial? Get ready to use the creative power of the Word of Faith (of the miracle you are expecting to receive). The Word of Faith is the one God pronounced when He spoke the universe into existence. 'By faith we understand the world was formed, by the Word of God, so that which can be seen was made out of which cannot be seen' (see Heb. 11:3 KJV Holy Bible, *2006 Power Publishing Corp)*.

God called a physical world out of the invisible realm. You too can bring the miracle you are waiting for from the invisible realm with a Word of Faith. A powerful illustration of the use of the Word of Faith comes to us with the narrative of the raising of Lazarus (see John 11 (KJV Holy Bible, *2006 Power Publishing Corp)*. This was one of the most dramatic moments during the earthly ministry of Jesus. Lazarus lived in Bethany, two miles away from Jerusalem. His name meant "the one who God helps." He was the brother of Mary and Martha. Mary, who was also known as Mary Magdalene, wiped Jesus' feet with her hair prior to Jesus' burial!

They had accepted Jesus as the Messiah sent from God and had become very close friends with Jesus. The whole family belonged to the inner circle of Jesus. When Lazarus got sick, Jesus was not there. He had fled Bethany because the Jews sought to stone Him to death because of the doctrine he was teaching.

Jesus was in Betabara, across the Jordan. In the meantime, Martha and Mary sent a messenger to tell Jesus about Lazarus' sickness.

Jesus heard them and said, "This sickness is not unto death, but for the Father to be glorified, and for the Son to be glorified through it."

Jesus was telling us that God was allowing the sickness for the purpose of having His name glorified through the outcome of the situation. Think about it—maybe God has allowed you to go through this crisis, problem, or sickness so that His name will be glorified in your life through the solution, the miracle that He will provide for you.

Jesus decided to stay there for two more days. Jesus knew that for the miracle to occur, it had to be the right timing. The circumstances were not ready for the raising to take place. Is it the right timing for your miracle? Do you need to wait a little longer?

Finally, after two days, Jesus arrived at Bethany. He asked, "Where have you placed him?"

"In a tomb," they said. They took Him to the tomb.

Jesus saw how powerless humans were before death. Seeing their impotence, He was disturbed in his Spirit and "cried" (see John 11:35 KJV Holy Bible, *2006 Power*

Publishing Corp). Their suffering moved Him. He felt compassion and empathy for them.

My friend, with the same compassion, He sees your need. God cares for you. He wants to help you—if you will only believe.

Jesus said, "Remove the stone."

The stone was the obstacle in front of the miracle. Perhaps, in your case, it is not a physical stone; it could be the stone of doubt, the stone of unbelief, the stone of self-sufficiency, or the stone of pride. It may be the stone of sin, the stone of un-forgiveness, or the stone of guilt and shame. Jesus is telling you to remove the stone—so you can have your miracle!

In a loud voice, Jesus said, "Lazarus!"

He had to be specific because otherwise the whole cemetery would have responded. This also applies to you and me. When asking for a miracle, we have to be specific.

You may say, "Father, I need a job doing so-and-so. I need a car of this brand (give the specifications). I need a wife as such and such. I need a husband as such and such. I need You to restore my marriage. I need finances for _____. I need so much_____. I need you to heal me of_____. I need you to save my son, so and so."

Do you understand what I mean? Imitate the pattern according to your need. Jesus called Lazarus out into existence, and he was resurrected. Go ahead and call your miracle into existence. Call the relationship into existence. Call the job into existence. Use the creative power of your faith—and do not doubt in your heart—and it will come to pass. Praise the Lord!

Once you receive your miracle, give glory to God. Tell others how God answers prayers. God will be happy with you for doing that. To reaffirm your faith, repeat these words:

> I declare that I will confess or say whatever God says about me. I will confess His promises concerning my needs and me. I will be careful with what I say because I agree with the Word, that life and death are in the power of the tongue. God will honor my confession and will give me the miracle I need because I understand that faith works with confession. Amen.

Secret XII

Faith Has to Be Filled with Expectation

The late great televangelist Oral Roberts had a theme song that said, "Something good is going to happen to you." He wanted to create an expectation in his audience of receiving a miracle.

There is a biblical example of mixing faith with expectation in **Daniel 3:17**.

Nebuchadnezzar, the king of Babylon, invaded Jerusalem with his army in 605 BC. He took the vessels of the temple to use them in the worshipping of his gods. He also took young men from the nobility of Jerusalem, including Daniel, Shadrach, Meshach, and Abednego. Daniel and his friends were great scholars.

Because of Daniel's wisdom in interpreting some of Nebuchadnezzar's dreams, the king held the young man in great esteem. He appointed Daniel as governor of Babylon and chief of staff of all the statesmen in the courthouse. King Nebuchadnezzar decided to build a statue for public worship. Anyone who did not worship the statue would be sentenced to die in a fiery furnace.

Shadrach, Meshach, and Abednego swore not to worship the statue. They chose to worship the God of Israel. The king ordered the service to begin, but the three friends did not bow before the statue.

The king heard about it, and he was stricken with rage and sentenced them to be burned alive in the fiery furnace. It had been heated seven times hotter than usual, but the friends said, "God will deliver us from your hands." They were expecting God to intervene miraculously and protect their lives.

The king ordered his strongest soldiers to bind them and throw them into the fire. In the process of throwing them into the furnace, the soldiers died from heat exhaustion.

The king looked into the furnace and asked, "How many were thrown into the furnace? Was it three? I see them loose, not bound, and I see four of them. The fourth one looks like the son of the god." When he ordered his soldiers to bring them out, the fire had not touched their clothes, hair, or skin. They did not even smell like smoke.

So they received their miracle that day. They were delivered as they expected to be.

When you ask for a miracle, do it with expectation. When you plant a seed of faith, mix it with expectation. It will bring about the miracle you are waiting for.

When you send a financial seed in order to harvest a miracle, do it with expectation. Earmark your money order specifically. Put what you are expecting as harvest, and the Lord of the harvest will give it to you.

Don't hesitate to have expectancy when it comes to your faith. It is all right to expect that your faith has a definite result. If you believe with a purpose—and keep a determined result in mind—you will receive what you expect to receive from the seeds you planted. If you expect nothing, you'll get nothing. If you expect a determined result, you will get it.

When the woman with the blood issue approached Jesus, she said, "If I could only touch the hem of His garment, I will be healed." She expected to be healed when she touched His garment. And she was. Let your seed be filled with expectation whenever you plant it from now on. You will receive your miracle. As you plant your seed, do it with a purpose and expect a predetermined result.

I want you to repeat this declaration of faith for the purpose of reaffirming your faith:

> I declare that my faith will be filled with expectation. I believe that my level of expectation will determine the answer I receive. I believe in a big God who is capable of answering my prayers—even beyond my wildest expectations. I know that God is able to give me a harvest, according to my expectations, in the name of Jesus. Amen.

Conclusion

I hope the time you have spent reading this book has strengthened your faith. You have learned that you can only have true faith if you approach God, believing He exists—and that He rewards those who diligently seek Him. You have learned the importance of believing with your mind and with all your heart or your spirit. God is looking for worshippers who worship Him in spirit and in truth.

You have been exposed to the spiritual truth that miracles may be instantaneous or progressive. You have learned that faith has two polarities: belief and disbelief. The stronger your faith is, the less you doubt or disbelieve. The miracle will only be manifested when you believe without a doubt—and when your faith is greater than your doubt.

You have learned that there are three milestones to faith: inception, conception, and delivery. This process is necessary for every miracle—and the Lord will be with you throughout the process.

We have also considered that faith has no boundaries; faith operates even at a distance. You may pray for people wherever they are, and faith will work the same. The Lord will intervene, and miracles will happen.

We have learned that faith is like a towel; it adapts itself to different needs. The same faith is required for whatever miracle you are asking from the Lord. Faith is the common denominator to all miracles.

You have also been exposed to the principle that nobody can use your faith but you. You alone can use your faith, and according to your faith, it shall be done.

You have learned that some miracles will not manifest until your faith is strong, you stop talking negative things contrary to the promises of the Lord, or you believe more in the Lord than in the circumstances. Any delay in the manifestation of the miracle could be due to weakness of faith, lack of forgiveness, guilt, shame, or a desire to impose our own timing on the miracle.

You have learned that sometimes you need to plant a seed to harvest a miracle; 'whatever a man does plant, that will he also reap'. You have learned that faith works with confession—saying the same things that God says concerning the believer and his or her needs.

You have learned that your faith must be filled with the expectation of receiving a miracle. The faith that works is the one that is expecting to receive an answer from the Lord.

My dear reader, go put these lessons into practice and expect miracles to happen in your life. Do not forget to share the testimonies of the miracles you receive to give God the honor and the glory.

I hope that this book has been a help to you in your understanding of faith and how it works. I will be happy to hear the testimonies you have from your experiences in dealing with the God of miracles. Feel free to contact me via e-mail at 12SecretTestimonies@Gmail.com. God bless you.

(Victor and his wife, Margarita!)

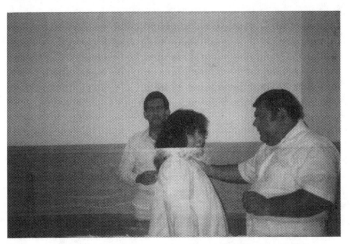

(Victor baptizing his daughter, Rachel)

Citation Locator

Chapter I: Faith is not Mental Assent

i. "For out of the heart flow the springs of life: blessings and miracles (Prov. 4:23).

ii. "For with heart you believe unto salvation" (Rom. 10:10).

iii. The Bible says that God created man in his image (Gen. 1:26)

iv. "God is "looking for worshippers who want to worship Him in spirit and in truth" (John 4:23).

Chapter II: Faith Activates the Mental Senses

The Rich Man and Lazarus: a parable (Luke 16:19–31).

"Now faith is the assurance [the confirmation, the title deed] of the things we hope for being, the proof of things we do not see, and the conviction of their reality" (Heb. 11:6).

"You will be the father of many nations." (Gen.17:4–5).

"By faith she received strength in her womb to conceive" (Heb. 11:11).

"Let my people go with me into the desert that they may serve me" (Ex. 5:1).

'But, you have not listened': 'Thus has said the Lord'; 'so that you may know who Jehovah is', Moses said, 'I will touch the river with my rod, and the water shall become blood, all the fish will die, the river will stink, and the Egyptians will be nauseated if they were to drink the water'. And it happened just like Moses said (Ex. 7:14–18).

"Only evil was in the heart and purpose of man" (Gen. 6).

"For who is this uncircumcised Philistine, that he should defy the armies of the living God?" (1 Sam. 21:26).

Chapter III: Faith Has Two Kinds of Results

"By faith she received strength in her womb to conceive" (Heb. 11:11).

"Can you see?" (Mark 8:23).

'I see the men like trees walking'.

Chapter IV: Faith Has Two Polarities

"Faith comes by hearing, hearing from the Word of God" (Rom. 10:17).

(James 1:17).

Mark (9:14–29).

'If you can do anything for us, have mercy on us, heal my son'.

'Is your faith strong enough to believe that I am capable of healing your son'?

'Lord I believe, help my weakness of faith' (NIV).

"Lord I believe, help thou my unbelief" (Mark 9:24, KJV)

"Who has believed our announcement" (Isa. 53).

"Faith comes by hearing." (Eph. 1:3).

"It may give the harvest of 30, or 60 or 100 percent" (Mark 4).

Chapter V: The Milestones of Faith

"The miracle happened, and Jesus asked, 'Who touched me?'" (Mark 5:29).

The woman with the issue of blood (Mark 5:27).

Chapter VI: Faith Knows No Boundaries

'I am a man under authority and I tell my servants to come and they come, and to others I say go and they go. You do not have to come to my house, but just say the Word and my servant will be healed'. To which Jesus replied, 'I have not seen such faith, not even In Israel'

Jesus heals the daughter of a Gentile woman.

Matthew 15.

'Have mercy on me O Lord, Son of David. My daughter is severely demon possessed'.

"Lord, Son of David'.

'Father why have thou forsaken me'?

Jesus felt abandoned, and he said as if the Father had the book of Hebrews call Him the author and finisher of our faith (Heb. 12:2)

'Dismiss her, because she is crying behind us and she is annoying to us'.

'I was not sent, except to the lost sheep of the house of Israel'.

'It is no good to take the children's bread and throw it to the little dogs' to which she replied: 'yes Lord, yet even the little dogs eat the crumbs which fall from the masters table.'

'Her faith was bigger than all the obstacles, objections, denials, theological reasons, and doubts'. (Matt. 15:28).

Chapter VII: Faith Adapts Itself to the Need

"Without faith, it is impossible to please God" Heb. 11:6

How was the woman with the issue of blood healed? By faith Mark 5:28

How was the centurion's servant healed? His servant was healed by faith Luke 7:1–10

How was the Red Sea divided? It was divided by faith Ex.14

'Go and stand in the temple and speak to the people, all the words of this life':

'Now Lord, look on their threats and grant to your servants that with all boldness, they may speak your Word by stretching out your hand to heal in the signs, and wonders may be done in the name of your Holy Servant Jesus': see Acts. 5

Chapter VIII: Faith: Once it's Yours, Nobody Can Use It but You

'Thy faith has saved you' (Luke 7:50).

'You will always have the poor with you, but you won't always have me, Matthew 26:11'.

Sight restored to 2 Blind men sitting by the Jericho Road, Matthew 20:29- 34.

'Jesus, Son of David, have mercy on us' So then, Jesus healed them.

'For with God, all things are possible' (Luke 1:37).

Chapter IX: Miracles May Take Time to Manifest

It was their doubt, their unbelief that disallowed them to receive the Promised Land (Num. 14).

Not considering his own body or the sterility of Sara, he remained strong in faith by giving glory to God (Rom. 4:20).

Jesus proceeded to reach down and save him (Matt. 14:26–33).

Sometimes we talk ourselves out of the miracle by making the wrong confessions and speaking negative words (Prov. 18:20–21).

"For if ye forgive men their trespasses, your heavenly Father will also forgive you. But if ye forgive not men their trespasses, neither will your Father forgive your trespasses" (Matt. 6:14–15).

"And when ye stand praying, forgive if ye have aught against any, that your Father also who is in heaven may forgive you your trespasses. But if ye do not forgive, neither will your Father who is in heaven forgive your trespasses" (Mark 11:25–26).

Chapter X: Faith Requires That You Plant a Seed

"While the earth remains, seedtime and harvest, cold and heat, winter and summer, and day and night shall not cease" (Gen. 8:22).

"Do not be deceived, God is not mocked, for whatever a man sows, that he will also reap" (Gal. 6:7).

'For out of the heart proceed evil thoughts; murders; adulteries; fornications; thefts; false witness; and blasphemies' (Matt. 15:19).

"For from within, out of the heart of men, proceed evil thoughts, adulteries, fornications, murders, thefts, covetousness, wickedness, deceit, lasciviousness, an evil eye, blasphemy, pride, foolishness" (Mark 7:21–22).

As you see, evil thoughts are seeds for the harvest of murders and adulteries.

"Honor the Lord with thy substance (possessions) and with the first-fruits of all thine increase so shall thy barns be filled with plenty, and thy presses shall burst out with new wine" (Prov. 3:9–10).

"One thing thou lackest: Go thy way, sell whatsoever thou hast and give to the poor, and thou shalt have treasure in heaven; and come, take up the cross, and follow me" (Mark 10:21).

"Give (plant a seed), and it shall be given unto you (your harvest): good measure, pressed down and shaken together and running over, shall men give into your bosom.: 'For with the same measure that ye mete (your seed), therewith it shall be measured to you again (your harvest)' (Luke 6:38).

'He that despises his neighbor sins, but he that hath mercy on the poor, happy is he' (Prov. 14:21).

'A good man shows favor and lends; he will guide his affairs with discretion' (Ps. 112:5).

'And Jesus sat opposite the treasury, and beheld how the people cast money into the treasury. And many who were rich cast in much. And there came a certain poor widow, and she threw in two mites, which make a farthing. And Jesus called unto Him his disciples and said unto them -'I say unto you, that this poor widow hath cast more in than all they that have cast into the treasury; for they all cast in of their abundance, but she of her want cast in all that she had, even all her living' (Mark 12:41–44).

Chapter XI: Faith Works with Confession

"The Word of Faith (the miracle you are waiting for or expecting to receive) is near you, even in thy mouth" (Rom. 10:8).

"Say or speak the Word, and my servant shall be healed" (Matt. 8).

'Obey him?' Jesus said, 'If you have faith, you shall speak to the mountain and the mountain shall move.'

By faith we understand the world was formed, by the Word of God, so 'that which can be seen was made out of which cannot be seen' (Heb. 11:3).

'This sickness is not unto death, but for the Father to be glorified, and for the Son to be glorified through it' (John 11:35).

Chapter XII: Faith Has to Be Filled with Expectation

"Our God will deliver us from your hands, o king" (Daniel 3:17).

The king starts looking into the furnace and asks: "How many were thrown into the furnace, was it three? I see them loose, not bound, and I see four of them, the fourth one looks like the son of the gods."

Bibliography

King James Version Holy Bible,
Power Publishing Corp., Macdonald, TN: 2006.